MW01174719

Astatine

Also by Michael Kenyon

FICTION

Kleinberg (Oolichan Books)
Pinocchio's Wife (Oberon)
Durable Tumblers (Oolichan Books)
The Biggest Animals (Thistledown Press)
The Beautiful Children (Thistledown Press)
A Year at River Mountain (Thistledown Press)
Parallel Rivers (Thistledown Press)

POETRY

Rack of Lamb (Brick Books)
The Sutler (Brick Books)
The Last House (Brick Books)

CHAPBOOKS

Winter Wedding (Reference West)
Twig (Outlaw Editions)
Broad Street Blues (Outlaw Editions)
Ottawa (Leaf Press)

Astatine

MICHAEL KENYON

BRICK BOOKS

BRICK BOOKS · 431 BOLER ROAD, BOX 20081
LONDON, ONTARIO N6K 4G6 · WWW.BRICKBOOKS.CA

Cover image: detail from *The Liminal Edge* by Lorraine Thomson
The author photo was taken by Lorraine Thomson

Design and layout by Cheryl Dipede.
This book is set in Requiem, designed by Jonathan Hoefler
and published by Hoefler & Frere-Jones.

Copyright © Michael Kenyon 2014.

Library and Archives Canada Cataloguing in Publication

Kenyon, Michael, 1953-, author
        Astatine / Michael Kenyon.
Poems.
ISBN 978-1-926829-93-7 (pbk.)
        I. Title.
PS8571.E67A82 2014   C811'.54   C2014-903873-9

We acknowledge the Canada Council for the Arts, and the Ontario
Arts Council for their support of our publishing program.

CONTENTS

II

III

IV

85 ASTATINE (A HALOGEN): the least abundant element in the Earth's crust among the non-transuranic elements, with an estimated total amount of less than twenty-eight grams at any given moment. Elemental astatine has never been viewed because a mass large enough to be seen by the naked human eye would immediately be vapourized by the heat generated by its own radioactivity. Astatine has been synthesized, since 1940, by bombarding bismuth (a post-transitional metal) with alpha particles, and is highly dangerous. The most stable of its isotopes is ^{210}At, with a half-life of 8.1 hours. The longest-lived isotope existing in naturally occurring decay chains is ^{219}At, with a half-life of less than a minute. At the other extreme, an isotope of bismuth, ^{209}Bi, undergoes alpha decay with a half-life of over a billion times longer than the current estimated age of the universe.

— gleaned from Wikipedia

Relation is not made up of things that are foreign
but of shared knowledge.

— Édouard Glissant

IN ACKNOWLEDGMENT

Before the noble gases, editing
the text, death of parents, matrimony,
*Constantinople is a very long
way from jazz*, last dance with onanism,

I'd like to thank Ashlan for Astatine,
Julia for the firefly puzzle,
Iain for the numbers and elements,
my sister the Sorer, her son the stone.

Lorraine for keeping it all together.

I

In the Hospital Grounds

The bird who sang youth now sings green old age,
the same sweet two-note call, one high, one low.
You are working *at*? You are working *for*?

This, for its own sake, my old handwriting
scratching *particle accelerator*
into my chart. Will that do? *Tu sei qui.*

Partial invasion. Improvisation.
What was outside is inside, inside out.
A man at a window. A robin pair.

A patch of blue sky. Doctors in a field.
The old puzzle of nest and branch and bird.
What struggle will take us from cage to air?

Song

A robin lit on the root of a fir
to listen to the soil on a thin
cool day in May, while from the topmost limb
the robin's mate was a blur
of song and I, in the least-lit room
on the fifth floor, fixed to a view, a frame,
contemplated our world, working a strain
of nether things: my limp penis, the pink worm
enriched by dark elements growing strong,
turning swallowed dirt into industry
for a tree to break its chemistry
into food for others to pass along:
scrap of blue shell, doctors in a stir.
The old puzzle of lift and drop and word.

Ciao, tesoro!

Who are you?

Sai, sai già.

Are you Italian?

Sì, sì, stupido.

Where are you?

Qui, andato.

Soldier's Note

stained paper
froth
spit blood

a coat
with deep
pockets

beloved
beloved
beloved

Above New Westminster

You arrive by chance and by design
on this hillside, retired and planning
fall, winter, deciding not to plan,
all round you in flux while you are still;
then all else still and you are in flux,
your new camera poised to capture
what else trembles on this fractured hill:
aperture and speed, dark and light, just
beneath, outside, next to the river
where air teems and clamours; look close now –
city streets, bridges, highways, sorrow –
and see, on the far shore, a little
stream that leads through a wood of old trees
that, if you follow, will let you breathe.

There you are. I missed you.

Sì. Anch'io.

Are you as lonely as I am?

Non è possibile. Ma, ti amo.

How will I get in touch?

Con mezzi speciali.

But you want me?

Sì.

Why? You want something?

Niente. Sono contento.

I don't know what you mean by "*mezzi speciali.*"

Sto andando ora. Mi deve. Addio, amante.

Active Pass / Milky Way

Shi'stle about to sound a white rip shore-
side of the beacon overlooked by three
eagles this last day of the year while ducks
flip in black smooth water beyond the wake.

I'm reviewing a voyage south, charting
another north so that pornography
will settle at the raw bottom of shame.
Bikers with haemorrhoids (the ward is full)

won't let me use the bathroom and I am
constipated. They are fucking nurses
in there and then streaming the video.
What can this lead to but the end of love?

Shi'stle about to sound, and a grey seal
rises starboard quarter. Sun through glass warms
my cheek. I'm reviewing a voyage west,
charting another east so a son will

find his mother and grandparents ready
to quit the village, last fires on the shore
(driftwood, old maps to ignite the kindling),
smoke spiralling a new cartography.

I'm reviewing future severed from past.
The old relationships. The bikers, not
the nurses, clean the mess. *Shi'stle will sound.*
Between the river of stars and the wake.

Perché questa guerra, questa merda?
Sei un poeta?
Perché non scrivere su di me?
Così posso vivere più a lungo,
come Beatrice?

Ahead, a Castle

I got to breathe by chance and, *phew,* nothing
could sustain me, no job or relation,
day faded as night closed, last of summer,
the building ahead a ruined castle,
night's sleep as complete as death, then loss-free.
The country lay at my feet, even though
the window was barred and the nurses old,
hushed morning over wet green patchwork fields,
room and stairs and kitchen haunted and chill,
doctor's room with a little dog and fire,
Mozart's *Requiem.* "Where, please, is my wife?"
No sense of what crops bloom on the far hill
or who invented the mechanism,
The Grey Sky. Distant pieces of my life.

Fragile

Che cos'è questo? she asked. *Pubblico o privato?*

Songbirds. A crow attacking a squirrel.
I don't know. A carpet of white blossoms.

Non ci sono nomi, etichette o tag.

How fragile is the thread that refastens
this morning to one four centuries ago.

Sì, riconnette. Che cos'è?

The old man's sorrow dying in his throat
after last words to his son, his daughter,
their words like ours stolen by the wind,
leaving a necklace of small hollow bones.

Sarebbe ossa vivere su un filo fragile?

Through all the mornings of all the seasons,
a neck-warm handful ready for wearing
as apology, as paternity,
as potential flight and potential song.

Non abbiamo tempo.

Familiar ghost weaving what makes us
human with what makes us eternal.

Nessun tempo.

As My Fist

Voglio che tu ricordi di me.

This meteorite hit our planet five
billion years ago, big as my fist,
older than any word or class or wall,
older than a coat of paint, older than
tomorrow, if you allow me some time,
older than species, maps and weapons,
Hitler and string theory. I am going
as its keeper to the collider mountain
I meant to forget: the tall volcano
of the foxglove, purple digitalis,
to toss it in, become a child again,
and (forgive me) forsake all I have learned.
When I grow up I want to be a king.
I want to be in love and have two kids.

Anch'io.
Voglio essere in amore
e hanno due bambini.

Bismuth

The definite thought of body begins
When writing and speaking begin to end

Va bene.

*

Il tempo è scaduto.

Below deck are slaves with their eyes fast
shut and up top the crew stretches, about
to start night watch. From the crow's nest the boat
looks frail and small against the sea; my task
is to fight off sleep and let go the past.

That girl treads water, barely afloat on
a blue ballroom floor, and waves windrow her
back and forth before she spies our mast,
our ship, our purpose. It is what she has learned
from her short life and from swimming alone.

Spring backs into winter before leaping
forward; the sea reflects sky. She will turn
and turn until my crow's nest watch is done
and I set this evening with the sun.

*

Rare, new, quickly found, weighed, counted and lost,
The definite body of thought begins

O perfetto.

Cranky

When we have finished with loss
what do we do with the valley
and the seasonal pond's
sulphurous whispering?

What do we do with the vertical transit
      from liquid to solid,
         from facts of life to facts of rock?
What do we do with absorption,
                      gravity?
What do we do with our subscriptions
      to *National Geographic*
      and *Nature*?
Well, here's a Cartesian well.

There are Darwin's bones.
Every button ever made.
Every buttonhole.
We need more light.

*

When I have finished with loss, I'll take
the chute over South Mountain
between blasted shale and blue elder,
light turning smoky,
quick view of my caravan, its green
fenced meadow, and climb out of the valley—
what I came to do—
climb out of the valley, fenced meadow,
its green quick view of my caravan,
light turning smoky
between blue elder and blasted shale,
taking the chute over South Mountain
when I have finished with loss.

Red

Eccomi!

Below deck we prayed then shut our eyes fast,
and up top the helmsman stretched, about
to start his night watch. He would steer the boat
as we went into our communal task

of sleep and might see you dreamed up at last:
a girl treading water, barely afloat,
reaching for a balloon while waves windrow
and buffet you backward before you cast

yourself forward. It is how you're keeping
yourself from slavers, men. *Sì, sono io!*
Now we know you harbour our survival.
Spring backs into winter before leaping,

and you flail toward the rising balloon,
drowning, not drowning, terrified, alone.

*

Rapidamente, dimmi cosa hai fatto.

Delta

On the day I came down to claim a wife
October was pale grey with a liver-
green sky and waves rolled high up the river
that shone, leapt and split my wilderness life
from farms, and as I crossed into the neigh-
bouring suburb's pools, crescents, signs and homes,
a panhandler spat, a child-gang threw stones,
a black dog barked warning then slunk away,
a housewife on tiptoe caught me staring,
planted her heels on the sidewalk and bent
to snatch her boy from my path, the school bell
rang and, there, a girl hung from the chain-link:
sapling, star chart, blood-in-cream wallpaper
from the fever-room I was born into.

Chute

I have finished with loss and with the chute,
the unstable valley, seed and sapling,
the bottom pond; one last fall perhaps, one
last visit to the silt-soft grey-silver
gradual liquid pull of gravity.

*

Sweet half-life, *O my darlin', my darlin',*
then gone, farewell, my darling Astatine.

*

Sono instabile, Astatos, amore mio. Ti bacio!

End of River Mountain

After the earthquake the army
quits, blown back by a bright wind,
and the battle dies, now near, now far.

Stag and doe kneel to drink and I
grasp the stag's strong forked branch
and haul myself ashore and break his neck.

For myself and for the girl, for all
brutal shame-fed bloody acts,
my wild stag's traded life is trading yet.

Ciao, amante.

Are you always red?

A volte blu, a volte giallo, ma spesso rosso.

Always so beautiful?

Sì, sempre bella.

Do you like our exchanges?

Mi sono inamorato di te, ma non capisco "exchanges."

Our meetings. Are they important to you?

Sì, sì, I told you, ah... ma devo andare, tesoro.

Hospital Grounds

I was born on a bright blue day in May:
Limb of an Oak, Robin's Mate, Blue Blur
of Song, Puppet in His Deepest Room,
Fresh-Cut Grass, Man Fixed to a Baby's Frame,
Please Son Don't Hurt Yourself or Others, Strain
Angel, Fox-Red Underthing, Wiggle Worm,
Adored by Dark Elements, Whisky-Warm,
The Third One to Come Between Night and Day,
Sweetest Breath, Rubber Head, The Robin's Dare,
Struggle Will Break Us Between Earth and Air,
One Absolutely Perfect Perfect Way,
Wah-Wah-Wah-Wah-Wah Wah-Wah-Wah-Wah-Wah,
Joy Itself, Scrap, Shelled Pea, Wizard's Garden,
Old Puzzle, Next Best Branch and The Burden.

Mower

Garden and lower orchard must be mowed
daily through May and June, also the paths
that cross the valley, the place we buried
the dogs and chickens and ducks. In late May
wet grass clogs the blade housing and I sleep
with my girlfriend in the marriage bed,
the cherry boat my wife and I floated
in for years, and it is strange, our arms
stretched above the sheets, fingers curled shadows,
paint peeling from ceiling cracks. Sex floats out

the window, the smell of rain blows in. Down-
stairs she paints the seventeenth century
on the dining-room table and we talk
about guilt and *duende* and happenstance.

The chickens laid seven eggs, I've not slept
a week in the same bed for twenty years,
I've stopped dreaming. And the weather! The sky
stupid with big fluffy clouds, meadow lush
with bees. Yesterday my neighbour dying
of cancer. Today, we'll see. I will cut
at dusk to give the snakes a chance to hide.

Grounds

C'è un problema?

There's a problem
with the robins.
Maybe the nurse.

Wicked scraps. Wee plot.

Living elements
turn, struggle, break out.

July Traffic

clutching a frame
in the least-lit room
I keep robins

in the world
in the spirit
in the flesh

on the dark landing
nurses twitch
I have swallowed food?
My bowels have moved?

*

Look! On either side,
stooks, bee swarms,
aftermath of the aftermath!

Near the Caravan

I planted an oak tree on my dog's grave
three years after he died and dreamed he was
trapped in a long-hidden egg cramped in his
lovely sleeping circle as patient as
he'd learned to be as patient as I wish
new buds and leaves to be red and fallen
and in seven years bare branches bare tree
white roots to wrap the bones and the dog held
the dog I held against my own ruin
birth immigration marriage loss and loss
shall be the dog I release and speak to
Géza up boyo and shake off your name
meaning it's time for us to shake meaning
God and all his friends and all our loved ones

Library

crowd the room they jostle cheek to jowl in greater
and greater numbers how do they get in? Small forms
interdimensional and vegetative they

squeak through lesions in our autonomic nervous
systems mostly welcome except they increase the
temperature and we must open a window

The dark is as welcome as they the quiet is
as welcome as they my boy is as welcome as
they perhaps it's how we name them *quiet dark boy*

On this side we know words so they must get to know
vibration and cursive while hospitals make them
microscopic and observatories name them

in the bottom of the ditch where old leaves collect
against a protruding root where nothing is bright
but water attacking softening spines and glue

loose at this point as blown nests for words that can't walk
to the mall or access the Internet too cold
and unstable while through the window we watch flakes

as large as tea cosies fall top right to bottom
left as we spin the collider counterclockwise
and catch what will catch nothing if nothing is left

Orpheus XVI

Look twice at the black dog with four legs.
You just saw a black dog with three legs.

Check the plant sale at the bank, your own branch,
all profits to lost animals.

When waiting for a friend who does not show,
enjoy the coffee, the red poppies.

Take the next Rilke sonnet to heart:
"You are lonely, my friend, because you are..."

Husband of a broken arm, take your time.
Joy is waiting. Joy is almost here.

Look twice at the black dog with three legs.
You just saw a black dog with four legs.

II

GHOST

1.

Overhead is wind and with it the promise of change. What paranoia!
I promise not to be late. You promise to be home. We promise the
kid a trip to Florida. Florida promises sunshine. Beneath the storm
above our heads is a ghost, a dark figure in a wet hurricane, the near
mad side of wind. Change promises never to change. Never promises
always. Always will never promise what it can't deliver. To live with
this, we divide change into bite-sized pieces. The inland forest,
where we build our hut, seems safer than the coastal rainforest. The
kid can walk to the neighbour's in half a day with only moderate risk.

While we wait for his return, we clean up, carve statues, have sex,
hunt for the next piece, if not the next puzzle. Our lives, what
collects in the corners, seem insubstantial at first. The boy returns,
shouting, through the tangle of blackberries, scratched and bigger
and needing a bath. Restless now, he stays a few years and, soon as
the path shows itself again, is off, this time for good.

You've seen the ruined hut in a dream, roof burst open to rain,
rain pouring through the thick barbed vines of the old climbing
rose, rank with black hips and new buds. The time you can't quite
remember or believe in, what happened between the first promise
and this discovery, awaits you in the hut. Bend low, the door is gone.
The doorway is a green sapling. Be careful. Consequence is at an end.
Events are coming. No holds barred. It won't be long. An old woman
on her knees in the cascading water looks for something beneath the
boards. Summer's that close.

2.

The trees are as strong as you are weak. The trees hunt, but not
in your time. Almost morning. The dew on your face ends sleep.
Others stir all across the clearing. Enough that you are together,
the last change come and gone, the thin signs it left thinner now, a
surprise at the bottom of your pocket. (Is that a footstep, a safety
catch?) The things you have accomplished here – the hut, the
orchard, the paths, three rough hills raised on your palm below the
new ring – all roll together in the valley you've circled year by year.
Chute. Elder. Chestnut. Water on leaves. And the faint arrival of
something that pushes all else away. To make room. Delicate, slight.
Porous.

3.

Ineffable. Wool. Sleep. Late. Black. Sieve. Sand. Dust wheel verb
run sliver wheel spin undone cottonmouth. Plantation, gift, loss,
fragment, skin of the teeth after birth moon monsoon gadget. No.
Special. No. Fever? No. Wholesome. No. Whatchacallit. Maybe.
Gizmo, maybe. Foxtrot, very likely. Hubris. Oh, probably. Ted
Nugent. No. Sibelius. Okay. Newton. Ouch. Darwin. I can't think.
Descartes, don't put the horse in front of the. Don't think therefore.
Crappy corny tacky. Spinoza. Moody Blues. Stones. Yes. River. Pink
Floyd. Yes. Pond. In a way. In a kind of round-about-imponderable-
guessy touch-as-touch-can come-as-you-may don't-freak-the-kids
way. Yes. That way.

4.

The veneer and crackle of what we made to make us safe (is that a
bullet in the chamber?) kept others out or in, in a kind of loop with
us forever at the centre — sinks with the last of the last sun and
we're in an ice age of slo-mo, all the dogs and parrots and chickens
and pigs wandering together, trying to pick up the latest clues, their
old brains still fumbling the millennia, the campfires, all the gone-
round rim of the possible, language a hook left dangling, syntax
roped by the short curlies and hung out to dry, once and for all, for
ever, I repeat myself, no matter, in the beginning, Logos, no matter,
till it's wild again and we start. Now.

In the city of X there lived a family whose eldest child, a son,
declared an idiot on reaching the age of twenty-four, decided to
live his life underground. His father, also an idiot, told mining
stories, spent the better part of every night in the crust of the earth.
Mornings found the family together before dawn, Dad just home,
Mother and daughters baking bread for the early market, the only
son one foot out the door, all the house mice and cats and clocks
waiting for the father's tale.

5.

The way they roll and seem not to, the souls, little stones making
a journey downstream, light on the river, current's inflection on the
surface, down deep, at the whim of the next eruption.

We work on one another in the big room on the west side of the
storehouse, only our breath and rain on the roof, regular gusts of
wind. A fish swims against the current (my finger on a stream point,
gallbladder fire), kisses the surface. A hawk screams and the bamboo
stick that holds the window snaps. A room closed is complete. All
planets and stars accounted for; the black hole full of monks, a
million bowing; and slightly to one side a traffic light flashing green
at the edge of town, and under the light a girl who seems lost.

She looks west then east: the blowing prairie, a gathering wave of
mountains.

A bird shatters the window, my little drunken moment – family at
the kitchen table, son eating beans, wife writing to the man dying of
cancer (he's got kids) – and all is in motion – wind, feathers, glass –
and all depends on what the girl will choose, east or west, though we
must not blame her for the way it turns out.

Pietà

1.

Here's a split, the valley cracked open. A fracture, horizontal. Why this obsession with direction? Up, down, left, right, what does it matter? Something has emerged. He touches his chest. From here. He holds the baby aloft and – look at her closed eyes, her face stretching as though she's trying to see something high above, her mouth opening – *Something to say?* Her fists float away from her body, away and back. Is he feeling a presence in his heart? Or: is his heart closer to his chest wall, trying to squeeze out, though it can't since the wound has healed, or has it even arrived? No, not yet. The baby's face is still and her body settles; see her weight drop?

The father is old, weak, and this child wants to soar. Her lids open and her black eyes waver and with the crack of cartilage his knees unlock and he loses where he is in favour of some place he has never been, though it's familiar. Why this obsession with the difference between *familiar* and *strange*? Why this small body? He looks up and the valley blurs. Birdsong swells and rain ticks on the roof. The mother smiles at him. *Give her the child.* She makes rocking motions with her cradling arms and he smiles and bends his knees and passes her the baby.

2.

The rift is in him now, like the horizon, part of the world he's always known but never recognised for what it is. He has swallowed the split the way the valley swallowed and quietly digested its own revelations. He touches his chest again, a Catholic naming the directions. Wallet and keys. Heart. Ticker. Muscle. Fist. How long will it take for him to read its language? Unbelievable, anyway. He didn't feel this when holding his son, or has he forgotten?

One thing's sure: the child bumping up and down on his shoulders brings an old swimming memory, a memory of when he was flotsam; or was it later when jetsam butted against the least part of him and his body turned into a swarm of fishes, a school of birds, a flock of insects, a murder of splinters, a parliament of flies, and he came apart, and the world was too numerous and likewise coming apart, and the long trip westward was done, only a quickstep into sunset.

Pyrrhic Victory

You're gonna arouse the anger of gods
by stealing from them that nice piano
you don't really need (do you?) since you failed
at piano – this seen by your ex-wife
and her husband busy topping the trees
around the house you used to share as an
apotropaic gesture, like knocking
on wood, so why not, I guess – point of fact
practise anything, who cares, it will go
well, it will go ill, because you're lazy,
and life is play, and play, *sub specie
aeternitatus,* is painful. Don't
use lightning when daylight
will do. Uncover the iris, I say,
so it may bloom another year. Open
the lid and play.

Reading *Middlemarch*

I just saw the trees outside Qualicum
and loved them, so took a photograph and
here it is, an effort at something
beyond my control, leaning, the lean mine,
a forest, a small forest of thin trees
just outside Qualicum where my parents
lived – Englishman's Falls, Qualicum River –
and I still love the trees, the photograph
of the trunks leaning, or seeming to lean –
I aligned slope with the viewfinder's frame –
an effort developed, mounted and hung
on the east wall of the outhouse in the
alder grove, and love this effort to sway
something beyond my control, the middle
of a spring conversation with my wife
in the sunny trailer, wind chime alive,
prop-plane above, called into this present
forest of alder with catkins, branches
bending truly, red tips flying, bowels
undulating, mindful of Casaubon
and Dorothea, outside our control.

Red

We travelled by night through the dangerous
slums near the bridge, the city overhead
bristling, you sick and needing medicine,
which we knew we could find at the market.

At the market supplies were limited,
the shelves empty, the place lit by oil lamp.
Neither the shopkeeper nor his wife could
understand, so you offered him your wrist.

You offered your wrist and the man took it
and read your pulses, and his wife gathered
herbs into a bag and we went away
and found a warm safe place with metal cots.

But all the cots were taken, so we shared
a mattress on the floor and lay awake
for hours under a dirty blanket.
You were shivering. I was terrified.

Wide awake and shivering side by side
we lay terrified on the thin mattress
and spoke and looked into each other's eyes
"Tomorrow," I said. "We will make our way."

Not long away dreaming of tomorrow
under the blanket, I woke to thin light,
a thin dawn, thin sweat over your body
and you were too weak, too pale, and I could

only watch you, weak, pale, your soiled fingers
hunting mine one last time across the bed,
knowing this was the final place for us,
the last place, last time, last shared thought and dream.

One last time your thin body resisted
waking while I watched the morning's long white
veins ride forward across the thin blanket,
and saw your eyes glitter, your wrists open.

Red Blooms

I stop reading a poem and take out
my unfinished story to write *flying*
over drowned valleys and mountains green with
seaweed on the back of the red-inked text.

These fall days teach me to split everything,
to dwell on isotopes, find new settings
for old arguments, to invest again
in the same solar plexus, knees, thighs, fingers,

unpack the greenhouse, seed the earth, loop
words to force shoots from foolscap, and muscle
you to return to this upland meadow,
to this hut, river bend, bridge, one last time.

Ciao?

Hello, angel.

Così in fretta, il vostro tempo. Così in fretta. Come posso dire cosa significhi per me?

I don't understand.

Se solo potessi toccarti. Se solo potessimo incontrare.

I...

Ah cazzo, il nostro tempo è finite.

ASTATINE

She is here. Sleeping.

Skinny young crows scream and scream.

I will not seek her.

Physicists meet her,

show her the damage,

the rebuilding.

They pray at the fire.

She weeps for the dead

on our small hill.

In meditation,

I look for accidents to

hurl us together.

"The grass is heavy

with seed," one physicist says.

"Sit inside her room."

She runs down

the mountain path shouting,

vanishes in trees.

Workmen shade their eyes

(unstable, dark, Italian),

drop their tools.

Seconds pass.

All the valley is quiet.

Sun through river steam.

Villagers

puzzle over mud, ankle-

deep in slime,

picking traces

from alluvium and laughing

as they fill their bags.

Her face, pale and slow

under her black hair, streams

with summer rain.

Che cosa sta succedendo?

Her lashes raised above black eyes.

Tu mi vuoi?

I step back

into the sunny doorway's

green light.

"I made a wish."

She smiles like a child.

È bello vederti.

I sit at her side,

watch her sleep.

Beautiful.

She offers me

Sto pensando a un cambiamento.

"This will not last."

We swim the river,

drift under dragonflies,

iridescent turquoise.

Shadows flicker

in bleached river grasses

against the sky.

Amo il ponte!

Pursing her small red mouth.

"Yes, the bridge."

Her face opens,

kingfisher's quick passage,

new moon.

The river,

the valley and the mountain,

first black, firefly red...

Mi piace il tuo paese.

A small pain in my side.

Plums ripening.

Così bella!

Tongue of mist over water.

Sun just risen.

She lies on her back

as sun climbs the clearing,

the overgrown track.

"No need to go."

Non c'è motivo di restare.

"But still."

Gli alberi di pino.

"Pine grove. The two of us."

I due di noi.

"And a jasmine tree."

E un albero di gelsomino.

"Gelsomino."

We fly uphill,

the pain in my side gone.

Sono libero? Va bene? Sì?

Clouds race,

bend over us,

slip away.

Non ti

scordar di me.

Affrettatevi!

Downriver,

red spinning

leaves.

SILVER BOAT

The Tao that can be told
is not the eternal Tao. (1)

All things end in the Tao
as rivers flow into the sea. (32)

— Tao Te Ching

through fathoms of salt water
without wind, no sail yet
this family is our silver boat
to the thin blue horizon

without wind, no sail yet
our dreams bounded by ripples
to the thin blue horizon
the same as the sun's

our dreams bounded by ripples
our path on the water
the same as the sun's
bow wave and wake, turn and turn

our path on the water
where we are going, where we've been
bow wave and wake, turn and turn
wave and particle

where we are going, where we've been
the sea big enough to contain it all
wave and particle
this family will carry us

the sea big enough to contain it all
through intertidal wetlands
this family will carry us
through estuary and delta

through intertidal wetlands
we will explore the salt and the fresh
through estuary and delta
and tides' calm moments

we will explore the salt and the fresh
safe under grey skies
and tides' calm moments
alone eternally and together

safe under grey skies
bounded by ripples, our path
alone eternally and together
the same as the sun's

bounded by ripples, our path
a river wild enough to sweep us
the same as the sun's
back to the horizon

a river wild enough to sweep us
our bodies our boats
back to the horizon
this family an intricate delicate craft

our bodies our boats
the love that sings through us
this family an intricate delicate craft
as the world is tossed

the love that sings through us
with the wind and a new journey
as the world is tossed
in giant swells, our course steady

with the wind and a new journey
this family is our silver boat
in giant swells, our course steady
through fathoms of salt water

Song

So what if this is a hospital ward?
With luck there'll soon be birds singing outside,
so if a tide of chemicals sweeps me
away tonight, I won't struggle against
anything except detachment from song:
varied thrush, finch, blackbird, starling, raven.
And faces, the last-loved human faces,
bewildered animals left in the car.
And pain, perhaps I'll struggle against pain,
the heart swinging free of breath, one more breath.
You are here, always now, face upside down,
seeing me; our unborn children are here.
They say a song comes just before death with
no time to sing it. Will you carry me
outside to the clearing we found that spring
where there played such a music box of birds?

III

Half-Lives

Some listen to children, some history.
The earth is full of not only what we
have put in it, but with its own beauty,
which is not terrifying, and then is.

The heart hears a child and listening
through the child's heart for the world
is harder than listening to history
or to trucks shifting down on Dunbar.

We rate half-lives but do not register
our own guts wrestling with beans and cabbage.
We fall in love with teachers, our stomachs
in a knot: *Sumer, Tigris, Euphrates.*

We dissect the giant squid, a stranger,
pale on the laboratory table.
Surely we should mourn the cousin we swam
with just yesterday or the day before?

We worship the earth and forget the sea,
yet ocean fills our blood, and a plastic
balloon as big as America floats
shimmering in the black North Pacific.

Once time and space are locked into a cave,
we can begin to explore yet one more
dimension. Plato, Aristotle, yin,
yang, echo of echo, iterations,

all isotopes colliding in our breath.
Perhaps. Listen. The steps along a street
at night. The steps along a street at night
are not the steps along a street at noon.

Song

They say a song comes at death
with no time to sing it. Will you lift,

will you sing before noon then lift
with *blackbird, sparrow, raven, gull,*

your face amid their bird faces,
the last bewildered animal, lift

with those you loved the most, lift
into the blue and carry this song

to a clearing, *wild rose, alder,*
strawberry, grass? Do, and I'll bring

seasalt, bismuth, uranium,
and we'll try something vital, quick.

Tara Sings

from Beograd to Vancouver, in winter,
along a fault line that began to speak
last spring, no, that began to shift ages
ago, before Aleksandra, before
Kenneth, a hot line of dividing cells,
each a girl with blue-green eyes who waited
in silence, darkness and the sea, for dawn
to open the sky and this new sister,

beautiful, beloved — "Who will you be?"
"Who will you love?" "Where will you go?" — till she
turns from the womb and swims into their arms,
a fish, a starfish, a startled sunstar
already at home in the world, a light
strong and steady as Fraser, as Sava.

Soldier's Note

Page found in bamboo forest.
Bound in ribbon grass.

Fifth month, plum blossom falling.
Hair white as silk.

Ninth of ninth, climb mountain.
Drink chrysanthemum wine.

Geese.
Geese.

Glass Finch

The pregnant woman looked in her window
at the bright room and saw no child, only

flowers in a vase, polished finch, sheepdog,
and the cold snowy night wrapped around her.

The man looked down the tracks and saw no train,
only his wife mourned, his kids sent away.

At nine, their boy is already at war,
a cub fostered, a lion enlisted,

his tank blown up three times in Italy,
three kids born, his wife buried, then a son,

his heart as big as the house he has to
vacate now he's ninety, the lit windows

turning snow into blind fields, *the glass finch*
cold in his large hands, his wife's once so warm.

Stoma

The stoma sits on my father's belly.
I won't be a nest for a crimson egg.

The red-winged blackbird hops on my belly.
My dad's colon purses its ruby lips.

His pale face above crumpled sky-blue sheets
gives God a bull's eye. Everyone looks old.

I can't concentrate, maybe want to die,
circle my wagons. Everyone looks old.

And now my father lifts his gown to show
my mother his half-full bag, the red lips,

last of himself he has to show. *Pity*.
She is horrified, he tired, both calm.

At the December ferry crows chase gulls,
and my mom forgets it all: pale-green gown

lifted, the wound, his black hands, tube sucking
bile from his gut, his eyes to the window.

The blue sky unseen through all the morphine
to ease his pain and hold his pain. *Red-winged*.

Above smoke and southbound geese (*crimson egg*),
his wagon is hidden in the night sky.

The Sailor Fell

Una storia del mare? Why not?
A stage resembles a boat. Something's lost,

mourned, every wave dangerous to the girl
overboard. *Sì, sono io! E poi?*

I'll build the stage, you invent the story.
Will you want rain, lightning, thunder, or calm?

What elements? Which war? And the sailor—
will he be in love, a foreigner filled

with gods, an exile crossing an ocean?
Indietro, amore mio. Calma.

Are you drowning? Will I swim to your side
in a chorus of dolphins, the sky green?

Indietro, amore! Shall I row
us home to our clearing where blue frogs sing?

EQUAL PLACE

the last proton hits

a crease in the light

that branch

nest, sister,

in your bare nursery

tree

sunstar,

help me sleep

the way home

low all day

we are *The Two*

wanting something

a stone in a bowl

Vi do il benvenuto

lightfast ink

frost undone by sun

slips from branches as fast

as you go

tu sei un uomo alto

silenzioso come il vento

quando tu mi ami

sadness

a trapdoor

to the underworld

oh queste tempeste

your storm, now my storm

devastare l'azzurro del mare

After Tu Fu, who in 750 saw census figures sink from
53 to 17 million following An LuShan's rebellion

heaven and earth are racked with ruin,
sorrow and sorrow, no end in sight.

I bend to the oars
row back into green land
eyes steady on yours

first light on black waves
new gulls busy with nothing
hands in your sleeves

shall we go hunting
before the wind turns to snow
and sea mist mars the sun?

*

the night's star-river
flies over my boy, my wife
ink jar between them

too beautiful
young man and his mother
heads close together

the shore-world empty
window open to fresh air
the gutter's last drip

his snowlit ranges
her snowy owl, wings spread
over the paper

*

I grip the oars
this tricky handsome light
will never catch us

rowing the black boat
outbound or homebound
just keeping afloat

Tu Fu witnesses
our hundred years of war
An Lushan rages

Pleiades roar
above our heads as we tend
north

Nine Lives for Dad

a sinking stomach
raven pair in the updraft
cancer and my dad

the left kidney fails
the right slows in midwinter
his hands turning black

a rising sky
raven pair in the updraft
my dad's Peter Pan

Fifteen Lines for Mum

The eighty-four-year-old baby climbed trees
to lie under the sky and read shadows
on the clouds; with the rain and coming war
she bicycled signless roads, Manchester
to Lumbutts, to a stone cottage; from there
she hiked to Gaddins Reservoir and swam
alone with the moor wind. One, two, three, four.

Swimming and warring are gifts uncounted
in the wealth of families, but we all
swim alone in the womb and learn to fight
long before we learn things we cannot do.

The woman born eighty-four years ago
has the same sky-blue eyes as I. Summer
days she hikes to Roe Lake to swim through dark
green watery layers: "So warm!" "So cold!"

Undone

Come regolare! Yes, yes: let's name
what we find. I'll go first. An owl stares down.
Abbiamo ancora bisogno di più luce.

IV

Discharged Moment

I was looking hard and then I found this,
the charged moment we used up when we met.

*

A wall against the body is body:
a standing heart attack: the mind wanders.

Introduce animal, child, a doorway.
"But are you going in or going out?"

The small suggestion of navel or eye.
Psychiatrist's notes. Commission findings.

Democracy out of chaos. This is
the heart-cry you gave me, not politics

but political, abstractions aside.
What did I give you? Brief music. A voice.

Bolthole, monkhole, secret passages sealed:
what else can a pathfinder hope to find?

The sharp desire to return if fulfilled,
or disappointment. This is where you live

and work: your estate, ditch, palace, cottage,
cave, enshrining every human dream

(I fill the inkwell blue, grind the glass nib).
When you wake from sleeping, will you help me

give air to the unspeakable puzzle,
begin again with standing wall, no door?

AENEAS

Perché?

Because, like me, he had three wives. Because
he was half-hero, half-divine. Because
he loved you. Because he migrated, Troy

to Carthage to Latium. Because he
was young and close to fire and war and
must know something of what is between us.

85.

Bismuth-bombarded after swinging round
the accelerator half the night (can't
find the light switch): pow pow pow, until you

are the size of a landmass, frequency
of clouds crossing winter land, exhausted,
whiffing heliotrope: hopeful results.

1.

He went out of the world as an ember
the roll of rich air an updraft
a salt-rimmed word, the father

he carried from flaming Troy
brushed off with the sparks
set down on his knees in Drepanum

Creusa haunting victorious Greeks
Juno's storm wrecking him
in Africa, in Carthage

to sleep a year with Dido
(Funeral games for Dad in Sicily)
to vault surf to Cumae

Lavinia's hair on fire
Father scorched by Zeus
Ascanius by unearthly flame

2.

Left Dido her gift-sword to
fall on. Saw his mom
Aphrodite, in the waves

Rose to the stars
Fell like rain
Rose to the stars

One voyage at a time
One war at a time
One woman at a time

3.

Seven billion years old
you greeted Apollo
with a handful of sand

Darmi quante più vite che
Apollo clicked his tongue
and you refused him

You started to shrink
The priests kept you in
a jar of crickets

of fireflies
until you vanished
in a whisper

4.

You were the first
to chant oracles at Cumae
A daughter of Zeus

a daughter of Poseidon
Aeneas called you
Sibyl, Herophile, Deiphobe

The Cumae waved
their burning scrolls
lit serious farts

You torched six books
sold three, said farewell
to the noble gases

5.

At Club Med Avernus
you took Aeneas by the ear
and named him

Jupiter Indiges
E facile di andare
all'inferno

You visited the Phlegraean plain
factory stacks, bristling
plutonium peep shows

the wordless place
where dead fathers hung out
singing about war

the Gigantomachy's
divine stallions and epic mares
The Going Down

horn gate of sleep
ivory gate of dreams
and let him choose

6.

Birds over the gulf
fell from the sky
stunned by your marriage

Sulphur and flames
burned your mouths
blackened your tongues

The Cumae affirmed your bond
as did the Tusks of Apollo
the Erymanthian Boar

7.

You were the Erythraean Sibyl
daughter of a Greek nymph
daughter of a Turkish shepherd

classic but sexy
enjoying the world below
(Apollo tagged your bones)

Amaltheia
Demophile
Taraxandra

You grew up among the Hebrews
the Babylonians
Egyptians

You predicted Helen, Jesus
the ruin of Asia and Europe
They offered you in the Troad

I believe if you
stop talking to me
I'll go to the wordless place

Macte nova virtute, puer:
sic itur ad astra, dis genite
et geniture deos

Etiquette

Ant rolls over and grasshopper nudges
her body, hungry. Wheat freezes. Full moon
and the hospital is full of wounded
sailors from the Pantellerian night.

The usual haunting of past by present.
Figures warped by time stepping down the stone
stairs, fluorine, chlorine, bromine, iodine,
astatine, ununseptium, and then?

At the Café

"You are kind of hunching, *ma perché?* Against what?"

"What?"

"Hunching."

"What?"

"Niente."

"It's you. When you go down into your rabbit hole. What I respond with. The waves adjust to the wagging geese, don't they?"

"Che cosa?"

"One father, two mothers, three sisters, four brothers, five daughters, six sons, seven grandfathers, eight grandmothers, nine nieces, ten nephews."

"That's what you hunch against?"

"Our populations keep expanding – except in Japan, Italy and one African country I forget."

"Sì?"

We're relaxing, arms spread. Summer on the piazza. Pollen-yellow sidewalk. Thirteen geese on the lake. Cottonwood fluff in the air. Everything (like her) passing as soon as arrived. What's the name of the song I can't remember which begins *Always...*

Who are we? Three hundred villagers massacred in the Congo. A family in Quebec dead by their own hand after putting out the garbage. She tells me.

That day in July we were between lives, the house sold, but we knew who we were. Spokes, radiating. Had our favourite south-facing table overlooking the street and the park. Smell of chocolate and coffee.

*

Today I remember cinnamon buns,
hot chocolate under Broadway awnings,
thick snow falling on the street, icy trams
snapping and crackling like aquariums
as we sank our teeth into cinnamon,
scalded lips on chocolate. Remember?
And then it was lover after lover
after lover, and then child after child.

I hunch over words. Did we have children?
Were we married? Outrageous passion must
produce more than its own image, mirage.
An ache in my left side, yes. She was born
to rebel, agitate, protest against
injustice, the rich brutally corrupt,
qualcosa di simile, wanted me
like my mother wanted, to save the world.

Swim Forty-Five

When I finish with you
the branch to the fence
a crease in the light
I'll finish with loss

*

She goes out early in the afternoon
now it's October, leaving my father
to dream the old dream of letting her go,
begun when he was a boy in England
and she a girl on her way to Russia
and the complete freedom she's still after,

stroke by stroke, on the rain-dimpled water
of Roe Lake, the New World facsimile
of her nineteenth-century reservoir
in the Yorkshire moors. A long swim from there

to here, watched by eagles, counting each stroke,
watched by beaver and ducks; she swims alone,

while Dad marks time and home: *she won't return.*

Soldier's Note

cracked a second rib
too beautiful

no way to escape
red-winged blackbirds

we are alive but
resist the geese

sailing north
wild kids tending south

the road home
aglitter with frost

the tea-brown sea
a stone

a baby's cry
snowlit ranges

someone missing
on a quiet winter day

the boy's eyes
sweet dark plums

in the tread of one boot
dry scarlet berries

you are gone
thank you

for saying
my name

East of Manhattan

How will the man with the broken shoulder
defend himself from growing older?
Italy, Alison, politics, Spain,
specific armour to prevent the pain

of the past from rear-ending the future,
his father's death in the cellist's kitchen,
the art council and civic election.
We sat in Donovan's bar in Queens, sure

of only the next beer, what can't be missed,
our Celtic wives; the day lagged and haunted,
held up by pylons of the Brooklyn Bridge;
familiar brother ghosts untainted

by sky, we were healed non-fathers, and well
away, our son asleep under the El.

THIRTEEN SECONDS

spire of white smoke

from the clearing: the hermit

building a shrine

herons fish all

summer deep on chopstick legs

their chicks asleep

sinking

raven pair, no updraft

caw caw

foggy sky

boat

water

poised blue heron

spoils his reflection:

our day divides

the crows call

only crows and people

only people

branch torn off

by wind or a drunk

young leaves still green

that quick path

up along

the cliff

still raining?

fields fenced to the horizon

sì, sta ancora piovendo

sparks fly

through deadfall smoke

fighting rain

Pleiades whirl snow

to the cove's

ice-cold sand

snowdrops

through grey ash

under the red-winged ferns

white spire

from the clearing: a ghost

quitting a shrine

Written on a Winter Morning

A dog barks three times. Snow is still falling.
Wonder if the streets are filled between me
and my old master. My wife and child are
gone to borrow winter boots, leaving me
alone with the poems of T'ao Ch'ien,
who stalked his heart away from politics
to a broken cottage under flying
clouds. The roofs are white this morning. I wish
I could fly. A fire burns in the south wall
near my writing desk. I wonder if I
am that dark figure braving soft white streets
to visit my old master. The snow deep
as a well up to the hill where he lives.
When spring comes we'll read poems together.

Winter Solstice, 2006

Dark times, my love, dirt in my fingernails
from scrambling out of the ditch. But enough
of me. You and Ashlan are the end, south,
close as bamboo. No smoke this close, all blaze,
just enough air to support light, your eyes
afterward calm. We'll rise from all we set
down. Like smoke we'll rise from tinder-dry nests,
from cedar, cottonwood, fir, set aside.
We are rich. We are earth, not fruit, not what
others see in daylight, but earth a few
will fall into when the footing is new.
That boy has your eyes, not mine. He will
fall and rise, inconsolable. I watch
trees burn, will always be consoled by you.

TRANSLATIONS

I

IN THE HOSPITAL GROUNDS

Tu sei qui?   You are here?

CIAO, TESORO!

Ciao, tesoro!   Hello, sweetheart!
Sai, sai già.   You know, you
already know.
Sì, sì, stupido.   Yes, yes, stupid.
Qui, andato.   Here, gone.

THERE YOU ARE

Sì. Anch'io.   Yes, me too.
Non è possibile. Ma, ti amo.   It's not possible. But I love you.
Con mezzi speciali.   By special means.
Niente. Sono contento.   Nothing. I'm happy.
Sto andando ora. Mi deve.   I'm going now. I must.
Addio, amante.   Bye, lover.

PERCHÉ QUESTA GUERRA

Perché questa guerra, questa merda?   Why this war, this shit?
Sei un poeta?   Are you a poet?
Perché non scrivere su di me?   Why not write about me?
Così posso vivere più a lungo,   So I can live longer,
come Beatrice?   like Beatrice?

FRAGILE

Che cos'è questo?   What is this?
Pubblico o privato?   Public or private?
Non ci sono nomi, etichette o tag.   There are no names, labels or
tags.

Sì, riconnette. Che cos'è?   Yes, it reconnects. What is it?
Sarebbe ossa vivere   Would bones live
su un filo fragile?   on a fragile thread?
Non abbiamo tempo.   We have no time.
Nessun tempo.   No time.

AS MY FIST
Voglio che tu ricordi di me.   I want you to remember me.
Anch'io.   Me too.
Voglio essere in amore   I want to be in love
e hanno due bambini.   and have two kids.

BISMUTH
Va bene.   Okay.
Il tempo è scaduto.   Time is up.
O perfetto.   Oh, perfect.

RED
Eccomi!   Here I am!
Sì, sono io!   Yes, it's me!
Rapidamente,   Quickly,
dimmi cosa hai fatto.   tell me what you did.

CHUTE
Sono instabile, Astatos,   I'm unstable, Astatos (Gk. *unstable*),
amore mio. Ti bacio!   my love. I kiss you!

CIAO, AMANTE
Ciao, amante.   Hello, lover.
A volte blu, a volte   Sometimes blue, sometimes
giallo, ma spesso rosso.   yellow, but often red.

Sì, sempre bella.　　　　　　　　　Yes, always beautiful.

Mi sono inamorato di te,　　　　　I have fallen in love with you,

ma non capisco "exchanges."　　　but I don't understand "exchanges."

Sì, sì, ah...　　　　　　　　　　　Yes, yes, ah...

ma devo andare, tesoro.　　　　　but I gotta go, sweetheart.

GROUNDS

C'è un problema?　　　　　　　There is a problem?

II

PYRRHIC VICTORY

sub specie aeternitatus　　　　　　under the aspect of eternity

CIAO?

Così in fretta, il vostro tempo.　　So fast, your time.

Così in fretta. Come posso dire　　So quick. How can I tell

cosa significhi per me?　　　　　what you mean to me?

Se solo potessi toccarti.　　　　If only I could touch you.

Se solo potessimo incontrare.　　If only we could meet.

Ah cazzo, il nostro tempo è finite.　Ah, fuck, our time is up.

ASTATINE

Che cosa sta succedendo?　　　　What is happening?

Tu mi vuoi?　　　　　　　　　You want me?

È bello vederti.　　　　　　　Good to see you.

Sto pensando a un cambiamento.　I'm thinking of a change.

Amo il ponte!　　　　　　　　I love the bridge!

Mi piace il tuo paese.　　　　　I like your country.

Così bella!	So beautiful!
Non c'è motivo di restare.	There is no reason to stay.
Gli alberi di pino.	Pine trees.
I due di noi.	The two of us.
E un albero di gelsomino.	And a jasmine tree.
Sono libero? Va bene? Sì?	I'm free? Okay? Yes?
Non ti scordar di me.	Don't forget me.
Affrettatevi!	Hurry up!

III

THE SAILOR FELL

Una storia del mare?	A sea story?
Sì, sono io! E poi?	Yes, that's me! And then what?
Indietro, amore mio. Calma.	Back, my love. Calm.

EQUAL PLACE

Vi do il benvenuto	I welcome you
tu sei un uomo alto	you are a tall man
silenzioso come il vento	silent as the wind
quando tu mi ami	when you love me
oh queste tempeste	oh these storms
devastare l'azzurro del mare	devastate the blue sea

UNDONE

Come regolare!	How smooth!
Abbiamo ancora bisogno	We still need
di più luce.	more light.

IV

AENEAS

Perché?
Darmi quante più vite che
E facile di andare all'inferno
Macte nova virtute, puer:
sic itur ad astra, dis genite
et geniture deos

Why?
Give me as many lives as that
It is easy to go to hell
Go with virtue, boy:
this is the path to the stars, son of
gods who will have gods as sons

AT THE CAFÉ

ma perché?
Niente.
Che cosa?
qualcosa di simile

but why?
Nothing.
What?
something like that

THIRTEEN SECONDS

sì, sta ancora piovendo

yes, it's still raining

ACKNOWLEDGEMENTS

The poems "Red," "Mower" and "Song" appeared in *The Malahat Review*; "Reading *Middlemarch*" and "Glass Finch" appeared in *Event Magazine*. Thanks to the editors of these magazines.

I would like to thank the B.C. Arts Council for financial assistance during the writing of this book.

Special thanks to John Barton for his sharp and excellent attention to these poems in the final edit. Thanks to Nick Thran and Sue Sinclair for their careful shepherding, and to Cheryl Dipede for the book's design.

Much gratitude to Gina Rota for her assistance with the translations.

DEDICATIONS

"Above New Westminister" for Alison Kirkley; "Orpheus XVI" for Jo Atkins; "Silver Boat" for Chris, Sadie and Dexter; "Tara Sings" for Kenneth, Aleks and Tara; "Glass Finch" for Dick Carswell; "East of Manhattan" for Rick Carswell; "Written on a Winter Morning" for David Roomy; "Winter Solstice, 2006" for Lorraine Thomson.

MICHAEL KENYON'S work has been shortlisted for the Commonwealth Writers Prize, the SmithBooks/Books in Canada First Novel Award, the Baxter Hathaway Prize in fiction, *The Malahat Review*'s Novella Prize, the Journey Prize, and both the National and Western Magazine Awards. *The Beautiful Children* won the 2010 Relit Award for best novel. He was born in Sale, England, and has lived on Canada's West Coast since 1967. He is a certified professional counselor and an acupressure practitioner and now divides his week between Pender Island and Vancouver, having in both places a private therapeutic practice.